MISSION DYSLEXIA

MISSION DYSLEXIA

FIND YOUR SUPERPOWER
AND BE YOUR BRILLIANT SELF

Julie McNeill, Rossie Stone
and Paul McNeill

ILLUSTRATED BY ROSSIE STONE

Jessica Kingsley Publishers
London and Philadelphia

First published in Great Britain in 2021 by Jessica Kingsley Publishers
An Hachette Company

1

The fonts, layout and overall design of this book have been prepared
according to dyslexia-friendly principles. At JKP we aim to make our
books' content accessible to as many readers as possible.

A CIP catalogue record for this title is available from the
British Library and the Library of Congress

ISBN 978 1 78775 296 2
eISBN 978 1 78775 297 9

Printed and bound in China by Leo Paper Products Ltd

Jessica Kingsley Publishers' policy is to use papers that are natural,
renewable and recyclable products and made from wood grown in
sustainable forests. The logging and manufacturing processes are expected
to conform to the environmental regulations of the country of origin.

Jessica Kingsley Publishers
Carmelite House
50 Victoria Embankment
London EC4Y 0DZ

www.jkp.com

Julie – For the late, great Danny Hickey – the original storyteller

Paul – For my mum, Anne, who kept my soul alive
with the love only a mother can provide

Rossie – To my parents and siblings for all the times they helped me with my schoolwork. To my teacher Mr Migilvary who was a huge inspiration in my young school life, and to all my school teachers and learning support staff from when I was older, who were kind to me and did their best to give me whatever help and support I needed.

Contents

A Bit About Us
(and the People
We'd Like to Thank)

Rossie
. . . .

Hi, I'm Rossie. I am the founder and director of Dekko Comics. I am very happy with my dyslexia. I might not have said that during many of my school years, but if I could go back, I wouldn't change it. There have been challenges due to my dyslexia, of course, such as finding it more difficult than most to read and listen in class, and to understand instructions correctly. But those struggles are what make me who I am today, and also what I believe fuel the cogs of my constantly buzzing imagination. Finding it difficult to understand instructions correctly can be a problem at school, but a great bonus in thinking outside the box creatively – once I learned how to use my creativity and odd thinking to overcome my school difficulties, then things got much better for me at school.

I want children with dyslexia to know that there really isn't anything bad or unusual about having dyslexia – as we're finding out more and more each day as more people are identified as being dyslexic. You might struggle at school if your school uses primarily word-based formats to get across information, since dyslexia commonly makes things difficult with words. But I think that's no different to putting people who can't draw very well in an art school. It's not that they can't get better, but it might not come as naturally as it would to someone who is highly creative but perhaps not so good with reading.

To parents and other grown-ups: I want you to know that if you are actively trying to help and be there for your child, you are already doing the right thing in my eyes, and it is more than enough. It is not your job to find the solution, but only to love your child and remind them they can achieve what they want to if they put their mind to it. The worst part of dyslexia, for me, are the self-esteem issues that can happen and believing you are a lost cause – finding it difficult and not understanding *why* you find it difficult.

This book will help because it was written by two very inspirational people (Paul and Julie) who work very hard to help people with dyslexia, and Paul himself has a very inspirational personal story regarding his journey with his own dyslexia. He understands what it's like to go through it, and has had a tougher time than some while still coming out smiling and full of wonder.

Together we have made the characters of this book (the three heroes and Mr D). This book explains the **strengths** of dyslexia and how you can use those to overcome your difficulties, rather than focussing on any negatives – although we do (and must) acknowledge the difficulties too, which we do with **Mr D**.

It's been an honour and pleasure to work with Julie and Paul on this book. I am happy to know them and have my name on this work. Huge thanks to Esme Baron and Sami Ross who inked and coloured the wonderful artwork.

Paul
· · · · · · ·

Hi, I'm Paul and I'm dyslexic. My journey through school was by no means smooth. I was labelled a "problem child" and told I wouldn't amount to much. How's that for motivation? There came a point in my life when I realized that I wasn't failing; I just learned a little bit differently from the rest of my class.

Sport saved me. When I used to walk on to the football pitch, I visualized the white lines as crossing into another world – I called them the "white lines of safety". On the football pitch I could be successful. I found school tough and left with very few qualifications. I became an electrician and worked long, cold shifts building boats on the River Clyde in Glasgow.

One day a lightbulb switched on for me and I changed direction. I went back to college and then on to university, graduating with a degree in Sports and Health Studies. I think I was the most enthusiastic, most motivated student they had ever had because I knew what a difference this was going to make in my life. I volunteered for everything – even becoming student president to make sure dyslexic students could access coloured paper for the printers!

I now work every day in football, based at the national stadium. My dyslexia broke and built me. Without it, I wouldn't be the person I am. I am a "big picture" thinker, able to manage big projects and build relationships and partnerships in the communities I serve. I can deliver a keynote speech with no notes and have energy to burn.

This book is the book I wish my teachers had read when I was my son's age. Maybe my mum wouldn't have had to fight so hard for me and I could have saved myself years of thinking that I couldn't do it. Embrace your dyslexia; you wouldn't be who you are without it. It really is your superpower.

Julie

....

Hi, I'm Julie. I work in education and I'm a mum to two bundles of fun and energy. They both have elements of all the superheroes in this book, and both face some of Mr D's challenges too. Bella is creative, kind and determined, and Shea is lively and hard-working and has a wonderful imagination. When all those skills and qualities come together, they are quite a formidable force!

Learning about my son's dyslexia didn't come as a surprise: his dad is dyslexic and they are like two peas in a pod in more ways than one. What did come as a surprise was just how dyslexia was going to have an impact on his life. Having worked with children with additional needs for almost 20 years, supporting countless children with dyslexia, I felt I should have been more prepared for the challenges we faced.

We have endured a myriad of meetings and a particularly painful school move, battled sleep problems, nurtured fragile self-esteem and had many a homework showdown. I often describe dyslexia as the fifth member of our family with all the demands, rewards and challenges you might expect from any addition.

This book is the resource I was looking for when I needed help to support my son. It's all the things I have learned and the things I wish I had known at the beginning of this journey.

My son is a proud dyslexic. He thinks his brain is pretty wonderful and I am inclined to agree. I have absolutely no idea how he remembers the flags, obscure facts and dates he can recall with ease, or how he can time that perfect run into the box on the football pitch. There is nobody like him and we wouldn't have him any other way. I would like to thank my family, my teachers and the tribe of mothers who always had my back: Jennie, Emma, Bee, Fiona, Sally, Lorna, Laura and Jackie to name just a few. Cathy, Lena and the wonderful team at Dyslexia Scotland are always at the end of the phone. I would also like to thank the wonderful gem that is the Strathkelvin Writers' Group and the brilliant teachers at Balmuildy Primary School, particularly Mrs Jarman, who picked us all up when we most needed it, and Mrs Kay and Mrs Claase, who helped Shea fall back in love with learning. Like all good teachers, they see past the challenges and help him to shine. You are all the real superheroes.

Introduction

This book, like all good things in life, is a collaborative effort. Julie, Rossie and Paul all have personal experience of dyslexia: Rossie and Paul are both dyslexic, and Julie and Paul are parents of a ten-year-old child with dyslexia. All three have delivered workshops and talks, written articles and taken part in training events in partnership with Dyslexia Scotland. They are passionate advocates for dyslexic children and work with schools to deliver workshops and training for teachers and children celebrating difference.

How to use the book

The book is designed as a practical support for parents, and teachers too – the resource the three authors wish they had had when their lives were touched by dyslexia. It is a resource that parents or other grown-ups and children can work through together to promote discussion and identify real, tangible solutions to the challenges dyslexia may be presenting at any given time.

The tone is upbeat, celebrating difference and diversity. Dyslexia may present some challenges for children at school, but neither Paul nor Rossie would be where they are today without it. The "super strengths" they have enable them to see the world a little differently and shine in their chosen careers.

Each chapter features our heroes – **Creatia, Willforce and Persisto** – who represent the strengths dyslexia can bring to your life. Together they encourage self-belief and persistence, and emphasize the need to use your strengths to overcome any challenges you may face.

Of course, dyslexia can present significant challenges, particularly in the classroom, and these are represented by the dastardly **Mr Dyspicibilia (Mr D)**. As the book progresses, you will notice Mr D shrinking as the child develops strategies together with their grown-ups to overcome the difficulties dyslexia may be throwing out right now and in the future.

There are lots of opportunities to stop and take stock, talk to each other, or write or draw solutions.

We've designed *Mission Dyslexia* as a fun and interactive resource for grown-ups and children to work through together, with activities and examples to open up helpful discussions, which can include siblings and wider family and friends, and find practical solutions that put the dyslexic child's self-esteem and self-understanding at the fore.

CHAPTER 1

Phew! We Made It!

ISABELLA'S GRADUATION

I can't believe I'm here. There were so many times I felt like giving up. Thank you for always believing in me.

Isabella

You've earned every step. You worked hard even when things were tough. We knew you could do it.

Mum

Of course, I didn't do it on my own. Can you spot a few of my friends in the crowd?

Isabella

Oh, yeah, I see them! Willforce, Creatia and Persisto were always there when you needed them. He was always there too, though, wasn't he? Mr D – if you look very closely, you will spot him too.

Dad

Yes, I see him. He doesn't look so scary from up here, though. Let's give him a wave.

Isabella

CHAPTER 2

We Are the "Heroes"

CREATIA　　PERSISTO　WILLFORCE

Hi, I'm Creatia. I'm really great at thinking up creative solutions to problems. I often see things that others don't.

PERSISTO

Hi, guys, I'm Persisto. I'm strong and determined. I'll never give up no matter how big the task ahead of me.

Hi, I'm Willforce. I'll encourage you to be the best you can be. I'll help you stick up for yourself and believe in your abilities.

There's only one hero missing here. Can you guess who it is? Let me give you a clue. It's the reflection you see when you look in the mirror. Yep, that's right – it's you! Let's take some time to think about what it is about you that makes you special. What are you really good at? Are you a good listener? A great friend? A talented artist? Top goal scorer? Do you love maths? Are you amazing at computer games? Are you helpful or caring? Are you a fast runner? You can't fly or turn invisible, can you?

On page 23 there's a space for you to have a go at drawing what you would look like as a superhero. Make sure you include all your brilliant skills and talents.

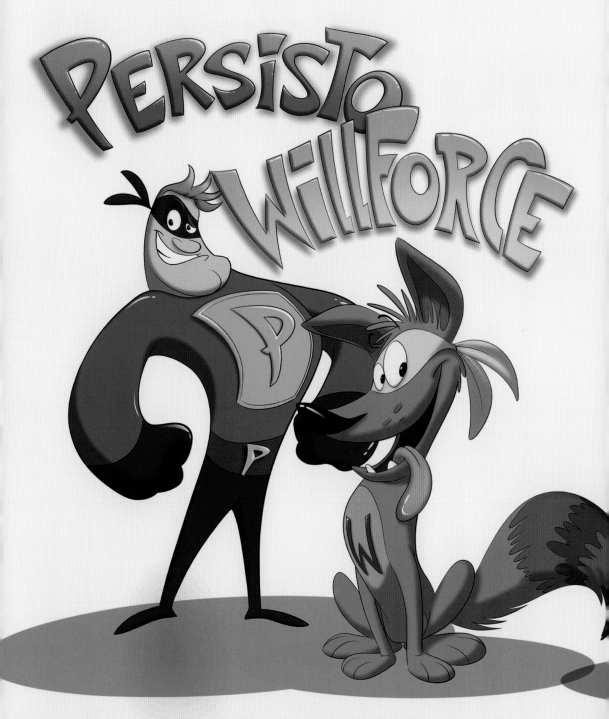

Guess what? We ALL have superpowers! Yep, all of us. You've just proved that by your amazing drawing. (You did do the drawing, didn't you? Don't lie to me now! I'll check. Oh, yes, there it is. It's lovely – good job!)

People with dyslexia are among the most creative, brilliant, imaginative people on earth. Did you know that? They tend to be great at problem solving and often think "outside the box", which means they are able to look at the world in a different way. Has that ever happened to you? Have you ever thought up a new way of learning something or a way to tackle a problem that nobody else thought of? Maybe you prefer to take things apart to find out how they work, or use your imagination instead of instructions?

Often, those with dyslexia are more tuned in to the emotions and feelings of those around them and are able to see when others are struggling or could do with a helping hand. These skills can make people with dyslexia really great friends, a strong part of any team and can allow them to stand out from the crowd. It would be a very boring world if we all looked at things the same way, wouldn't it?

People with dyslexia have loads of strengths. Creatia, Willforce and Persisto will highlight just a few of them.

I am great at thinking of new ideas. Like many people with dyslexia, I am good at thinking "outside the box", coming up with new ideas or ways of working that are a bit different. It's boring doing things the same all the time, isn't it? My ideas often lead to new ways of doing things or brand-new projects or ideas. I like standing out from the crowd and learning new things in my own way. Lots of entrepreneurs and business starters have dyslexia.

I am really good at visual thinking. This means I can picture ideas or projects in my head. Do you do that? People who are good at visual thinking make great engineers, architects, sports coaches or project managers. It's a really valuable skill to have.

I love completing jobs with my hands: fixing things, solving problems and understanding how things work. I also like trying to think up more efficient or effective ways of getting things done – often without needing the instructions!

I pride myself on being a good friend. I care about how others feel and like to help them recognize what they are good at. People with dyslexia can be very tuned in to other people's emotions and feelings. This means they not only make great friends but are often very good at meeting and speaking to people. Like me, they often find it easy to relate to other people, helping them to work with others, pass on information, persuade people and be aware when people need help.

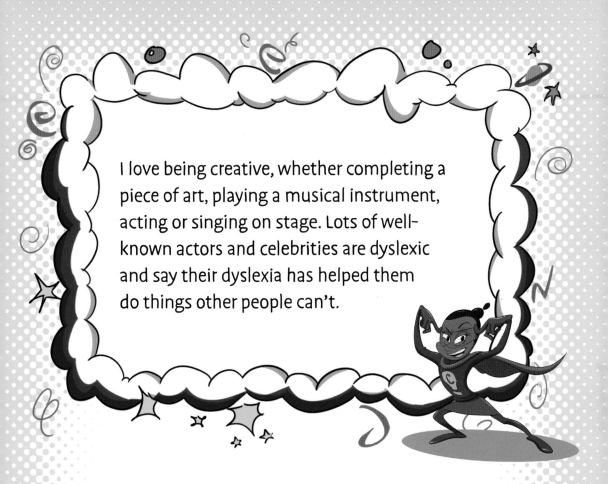

I love being creative, whether completing a piece of art, playing a musical instrument, acting or singing on stage. Lots of well-known actors and celebrities are dyslexic and say their dyslexia has helped them do things other people can't.

Many brilliant sportsmen and sportswomen are dyslexic. How do you think they time that perfect run into the box, work out when to increase their speed in a race, visualize a goal or perfect that rainbow flick?

That all sounds brilliant, doesn't it? Can you recognize some of your own skills and abilities?

Why don't you try filling them in on page 29, so you can look back on them when you need to remind yourself of all the things you do really well? You could even make a colourful poster of them to put on your wall at home. Maybe your family, friends or teachers would like to add to your list the things they know about your strengths? Sometimes other people recognize our strengths before we do. Have you ever noticed that?

Wow! That looks great. You clearly have lots things you already do really well. So when are we going to get a call from Hollywood to star in their next multi-million-pound movie, or picture the perfect run into the box to curve the ball into the top corner in the FA Cup Final?

The trouble is, our brains can be a bit annoying sometimes and tend to focus on the stuff we can't yet do, instead of the stuff we are already really good at. Do you ever find that? Sometimes it can be hard to think of things you can do really well, but really easy to see strengths in others. Sometimes we just need to shake things up and remind ourselves to focus on the positives and use our awesome strengths to our advantage.

OK, so that sounds easy, right? Just shake things up. So how do we do that? Can you think of any ways to focus on the positives? Well, making a list or picture as you've done is a good start. Remember to look back over this when you are having a day where you are struggling with something.

I'm not saying it's always easy. I bet it doesn't feel easy when you're struggling to spell the word the rest of the class seems able to do without a problem, or when your teacher asks you to read out loud and you can feel yourself trying to sink under the desk and become invisible.

"Me? Oh, no, 'me' is at the toilet just now! Move on, please."

That doesn't work, by the way. But if reading aloud is hard, then ask a grown-up or teacher for help and come up with a plan so you are not singled out in the classroom.

What about when you forget your homework bag, or only bring one sock home from PE class? Socks are overrated, right? Joking, I love socks! Just not the smelly kind.

The truth is that you are not alone. Many people who have dyslexia face big challenges every day. It helps to remind yourself that you are not alone. Everybody has their own strengths and challenges, and the best thing we can all do is to offer a helping hand where it is needed. Who do you ask when you need help? Are you good at helping others when you see they are struggling with something?

There are always people who need your help, and there are always people you can rely on to help you. That's teamwork, and we know Mr D *hates* teamwork. We will hear more about him in the next chapter.

The good news is there is already loads of stuff you are really brilliant at. This book will help you to recognize all the wonderful gifts you already have and find ways to deal with some of the things that may be more challenging because of your dyslexia.

Creatia, Willforce and Persisto are going to help you find a way to unlock all the best bits in that wonderful brain of yours and let you, and your dyslexia, take over the world... OK, take over the classroom. No, maybe your teacher wouldn't like that. Take over your bedroom? Let's start small, eh?

CHAPTER 3

Mr D!

Now that we have identified all of your fabulous strengths and know where to go if we need to ask for help, I suppose it might be time to introduce this guy. You might have spotted him lurking on the pages of the previous chapters.

I'll let Creatia, Willforce and Persisto tell you a bit more about him.

Don't forget to look out for him in each of the chapters and see if you can work out what is happening to him as the book progresses.

Look, let's face the tough stuff head-on. There's no point at all in hiding it. Although having dyslexia can give you all these awesome skills and abilities, it can sometimes be challenging too. It can affect the way you read, write, remember or understand things.

Phew, you're just telling them about dyslexia. I thought you were going to tell them about...

So, on that note I'd like to introduce you to Mr ~~Dyspic~~, ~~Dispica~~, ~~Dyslpice~~, ~~Dyspicy~~ ... ~~Dyspicibilia~~ – wow, that's a difficult name. Let's try sounding it out: Dis-pic-i-bil-i-a – phew! I tell you what, let's just call him Mr D! It's not just Mr D's name that's tricky either.

You did it, you actually did it! Oh no! Here he comes now...

Hello, you tiny, rubbish little people. My name is Dyspicibilia. Mr Dyspicibilia! Don't you dare laugh at my name! Are you laughing? I'll remember that! Let me ask you this: do you ever find yourself running out of time? Or staring out of the classroom window?

What about when you are trying to stop the letters doing a big wobbly dance across the page when you're trying to read? Yes? Well, I will let you into a secret: that's all me! Ha ha ha ha ha. Bet you are not laughing now! I love it when you can't find your place in a book, I laugh when you forget your pencil case and I positively dance with glee when you run out of time to finish your work. The more frustrated you get, the more powerful I become. And I LOVE being powerful.

To be honest, Mr D is a big pain in the bum. He didn't hear me say that, did he? No, it's fine – he's too busy admiring himself in the mirror. He loves to make things seem much harder than they really are.

On the next page, can you fill in the splats from Mr D's hat with anything annoying, either at school or at home, that you feel you might like a bit of superhero help with?

This can be anything from finding it hard to write for a long time, spelling, concentrating, time keeping, forgetting names or taking the wrong shoes for PE – anything at all.

Put each one in a yucky splat. If it helps, you can talk to your grown-up or teacher about this first. Sometimes grown-ups have good ideas too, you know. See what you can come up with.

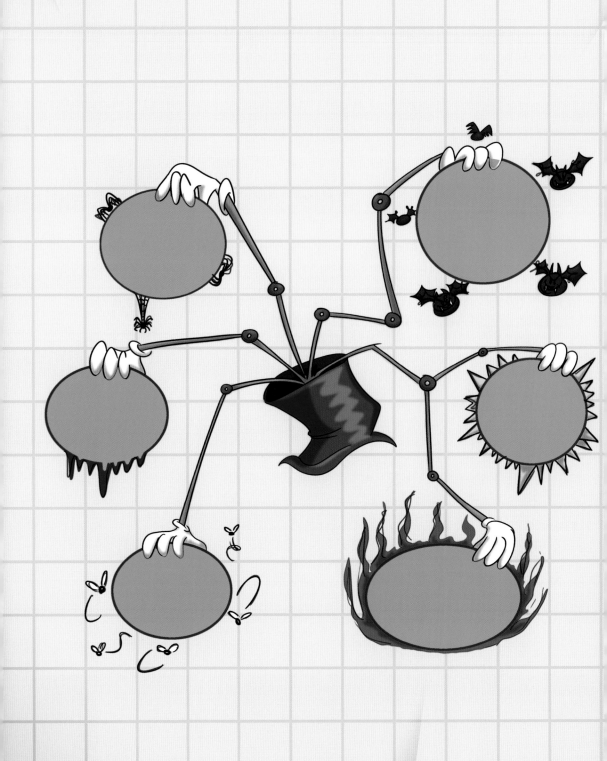

Thanks for doing that. In the next few chapters we will look at ways to deal with these challenges and get rid of Mr D.

CHAPTER 4

Time's Up!

Now, if you're anything like me, telling the time can be a little bit tricky, and don't get me started on getting to places at the right time or completing tests before the bell goes for lunch.

Does this ever happen to you?

Mr D loves time – he steals it just for fun. He can keep your mind so focussed on how long you've got left that you sometimes can't even get started at all. Or sometimes he distracts you so much with something completely unrelated to the task that the time passes all by itself. I bet you are an expert in looking out of the classroom window, aren't you?

Do you ever find yourself so focussed on which order to do things in that you can't get started at all?

Mr D loves to do this in tests. He makes sure you get all your pens, rulers and pencils in the right order, move your chair in, count how many birds you can see out of the window, plan what to have for lunch, read the question... All of a sudden 20 minutes have passed and everyone else has finished!

Time is tricky! There are lots of reasons why it presents a challenge for people with dyslexia.

Yes, it could be to do with the way you process information – that's how you read or hear the instructions somebody gives to you. That's what happens to me.

Some people with dyslexia prefer instructions to be broken down, instead of receiving all the information at once. Maybe that's you? Do you find it easier when you are asked to do one thing at a time?

Do you ever struggle with time disappearing? I know I've got 30 minutes, but when I look up, I've only got five left and I've no idea where the other 25 have gone!

Some people prefer to be able to see how much time they have left – there are lots of great visual timers or countdown clocks that can be set to light up when half or all your time is up. Maybe that's you? Would it help to have a timer that flashed green, orange or red to let you know when time is counting down?

Actually, you're right, Creatia. I always have extra time to complete tasks for this reason. You might be allowed some extra time, or somebody to write for you or read the questions for tests. Make sure you speak to your school about this.

The truth is that different strategies will work for different people. Find out what works best for you and use it. This will be particularly helpful later in life when you are working towards exams or planning your day at school or work. Forgetting to plan or not asking for help are the most common reasons to run out of time. Remember to work with your teacher or grown-up to make sure you have planned out enough time to complete tasks – and think about time for breaks if you need them.

The most important thing to do where time is concerned is breathe. Sounds obvious, doesn't it?

When you have a task or a job to do, the first thing you should do is take a deep breath.

Then check you understand what you have to do.

NEVER be embarrassed to ask questions or clarify what it is you have to do.

If you start to worry or panic, then you can waste a lot of time thinking about how much time you have and not a lot of time doing the actual task.

Next, work out a strategy for keeping to time. You can speak to a grown-up about whether somebody could keep an eye on the clock for you and prompt you to move on at the right time. Or maybe you would prefer to have a countdown clock or stopwatch to keep track of the time yourself. These strategies are for you – it doesn't matter what works for anyone else. Be kind to yourself. If you only manage to write two sentences but have come up with ten great ideas, then that's OK. The most important thing to remember is don't give up! Mr D loves it when we give up and we want to keep him the size of a pea, don't we?

Why don't you try breaking your clock up into coloured sections? Colour is a great way to break things down and can really help to chunk things into more manageable pieces. The most important thing to do is practise. Hard work will always pay off. Practise every day, working out what time bedtime is, what time you eat your lunch or what time it will be when you finish your homework. The more you practise and come up with a way that works for you, the easier it will become – I promise!

The last thing to remember is that you are much, much more than a score on a test.

Tests are often a way for teachers to see how well they are helping you to learn or a useful way of looking for things they could help with, not a measure of how clever you are.

If things don't go to plan, then dust yourself off, think about what worked and what didn't, and get ready to try again the next time.

You will learn more from the times you fall down than from all the times you did something easily.

Willforce, Persisto and Creatia put their heads together to come up with some great strategies to get time back under their control.

1. Get a good night's sleep. Bet you've been told that before. It really is so important to let your body and brain relax and recover before you tackle all the challenges life throws at you.

2. Work hard. I know you're doing that already. Believe in yourself and continue to try your best.

3. Break things down into manageable chunks. Don't try to learn everything in one night. It helps to read over your jotters or notes every day so it's all fresh in your mind. Take small sections and focus on one at a time so you don't feel overwhelmed.

4. Highlight any difficulties and ask for help at the time. If you are at home, make a note and take it with you to school the next day if you need help from your teacher. It's their job to help you to learn – remember this.

5. Use your strengths (and we already know you have loads of those). Can you turn the subject into something you find more appealing? A comic? A song? A different colour for facts or dates? Maybe making famous faces into football cards? Whatever works for you.

Tips for Time

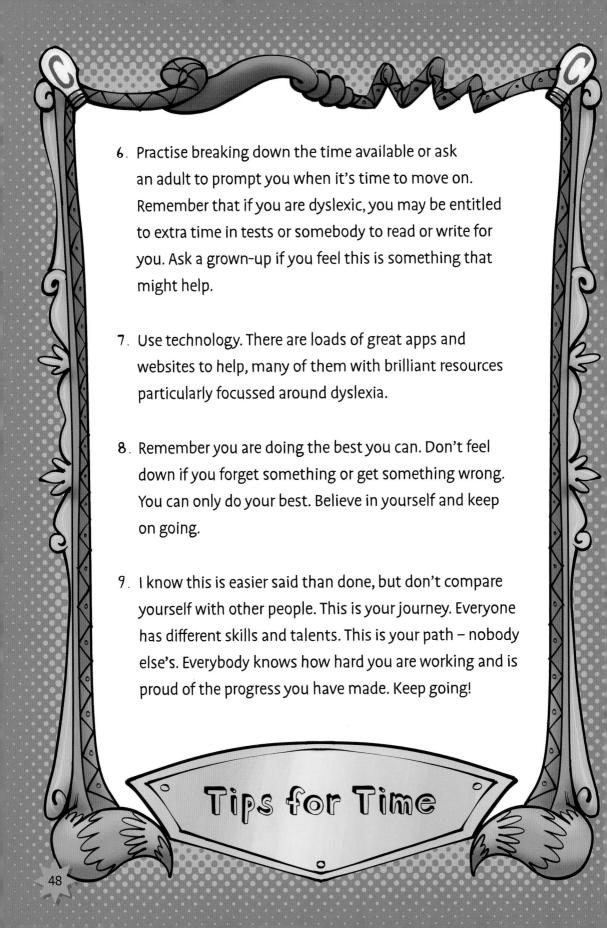

6. Practise breaking down the time available or ask an adult to prompt you when it's time to move on. Remember that if you are dyslexic, you may be entitled to extra time in tests or somebody to read or write for you. Ask a grown-up if you feel this is something that might help.

7. Use technology. There are loads of great apps and websites to help, many of them with brilliant resources particularly focussed around dyslexia.

8. Remember you are doing the best you can. Don't feel down if you forget something or get something wrong. You can only do your best. Believe in yourself and keep on going.

9. I know this is easier said than done, but don't compare yourself with other people. This is your journey. Everyone has different skills and talents. This is your path – nobody else's. Everybody knows how hard you are working and is proud of the progress you have made. Keep going!

Tips for Time

As Creatia, Willforce and Persisto have shown you, there are lots of ways you can tackle the difficulties around time.

This could be difficulties around keeping to time or something else such as reading the clock.

We are all different – the world would be very boring if we were all the same – so it is important to find solutions that work for you.

Have a look at the next three pages.

First read about what Creatia and Willforce find tricky about time and then write on the next page (grown-ups can help here) anything you find hard such as running out of time, being surprised when something comes to an end or working out what time it is on a clock.

Then complete the super "Time" hero. What colour are they? What is their special skill?

If you like, you can then draw your very own superhero to fight the challenges you wrote down. What special powers do they have? A pause button? A printer? A countdown light? You decide.

If, like many dyslexics, you think in pictures, this activity is spot on for you. You might even surprise yourself with a new idea you didn't have until you started drawing.

TIME...

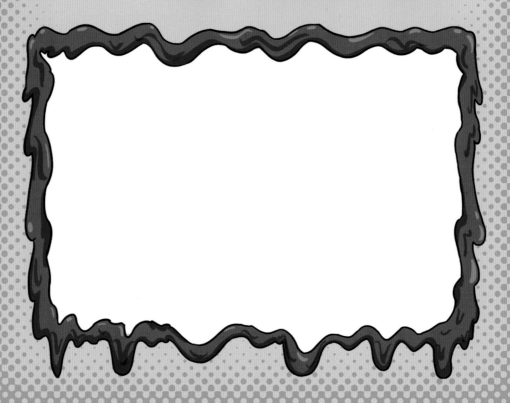

Was that fun? Show your drawings to a friend or family member, or your teacher, and talk them through their powers, if you'd like to.

Look, Mr D has shrunk a bit already!

CHAPTER 5

Words, Words, Words

Just like time in the previous chapter, words and numbers can be a bit of a nightmare. Words are everywhere. Especially in school!

Chances are that if you are dyslexic, words will probably cause you challenges in at least one aspect of your life.

You might be a great reader but struggle to remember a joke.

You might be great at speaking aloud but struggle to get your ideas down on paper.

You might sit in class and have absolutely no idea why everyone suddenly knows what the teacher has asked them to do and you don't.

Sound familiar?

There can be many ways in which words can be a challenge for people with dyslexia. Here are just a few.

Reading

I really struggle with reading. Sometimes the words jump around, sometimes the end of one word runs in to the start of another. Other times I can be so focussed on reading and understanding the words that making sense of the story becomes impossible.

I love listening to stories and really enjoy looking at books with facts in them where the information is broken up into smaller chunks.

How about you? Do you like reading? Is there anything you find hard? Do you have a favourite book? Have a chat with your grown-up and write or draw your thoughts in the spaces on the next two pages.

56

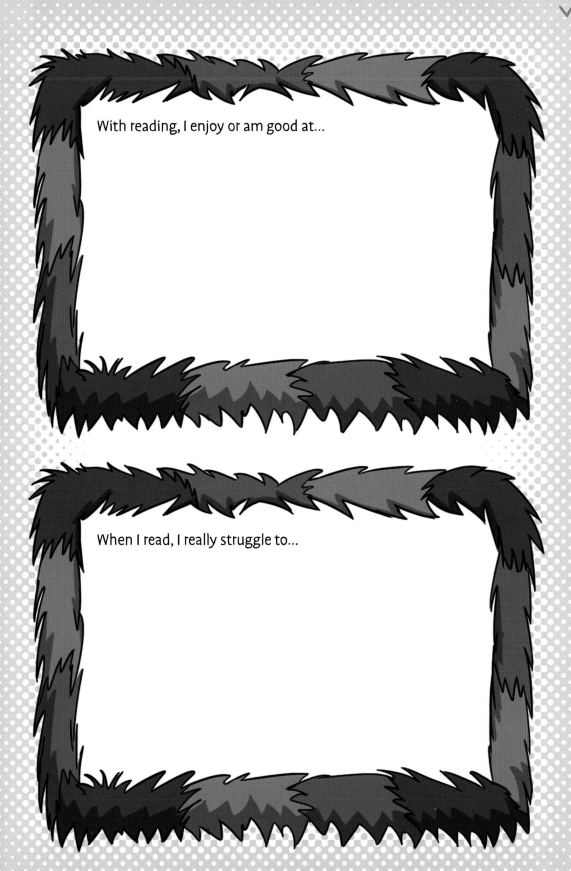

With reading, I enjoy or am good at...

When I read, I really struggle to...

Reading would be easier if...

What I want teachers or grown-ups to
know about how reading is for me

Writing

We all know I am not frightened to try hard, but that pencil just will not do what I need it to do.

The letters often form perfectly in my head, then come out the end of the pencil in the wrong order or all different sizes.

My hand gets tired and even aches sometimes, and it gets so frustrating that I feel like giving up. Forming letters, mixing up letters – b, d and p are particularly tricky.

Do you find writing easy or hard? Do you enjoy using your imagination and coming up with stories or do you prefer to copy things down from the board or a book?

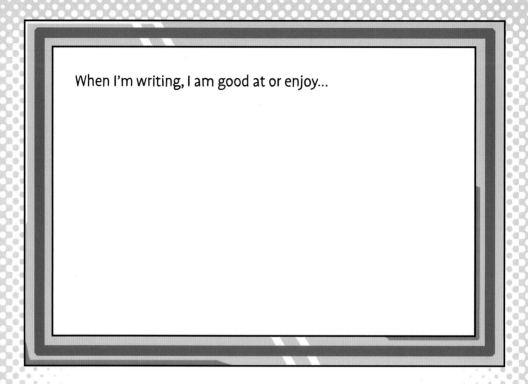

When I'm writing, I am good at or enjoy…

When I'm writing, I really struggle with…

Writing would be easier if...

What I want teachers or grown-ups to know about how writing is for me

Spelling

So who invented phonics anyway? Sounding out and breaking down words is really challenging for me. It's lucky I've got such a great visual memory because I literally remember the shape of every word – kind of like looking at a picture.

This can be tricky when I come across new words for the first time as it requires much more effort and much more space in my brain to remember all the different patterns.

So maybe you love spelling. Maybe you have a brilliant memory or are great at sounding things out. Maybe you find it really tricky like Creatia. Do you know any songs, rhymes or tips to help you remember tricky words?

For spelling, I enjoy or am good at...

When I learn spellings, I really struggle to...

Spelling would be easier if...

What I want teachers or grown-ups to know about how spelling is for me

Listening

Did somebody say something? Only kidding! Dyslexia does not affect your ability to hear, but it can affect the way you receive information.

The difference between the instructions a person gives and the information somebody receives or understands is not always the same. I really struggle with this in class.

Sometimes I only hear the first thing on a list of instructions and everyone else is on to step two or three. I really need instructions broken down into smaller steps and for someone to check my understanding.

Lots of people with dyslexia are good listeners, but many find it tricky to remember a big, long list of instructions. What about you? Is there anything you find really helps you to remember everything?

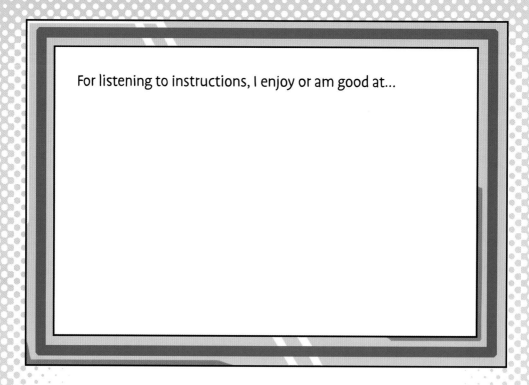

For listening to instructions, I enjoy or am good at...

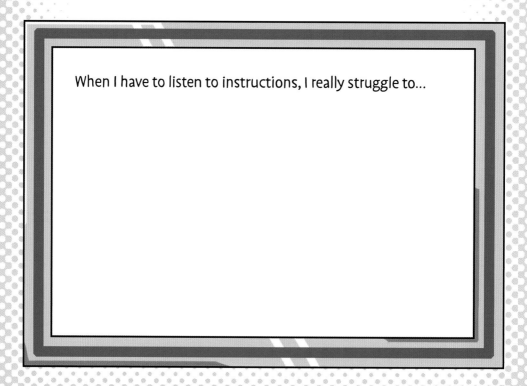

When I have to listen to instructions, I really struggle to...

Listening to instructions would be easier if...

What I want teachers or grown-ups to know about how listening to instructions is for me

Reading aloud

Sometimes I don't feel confident reading out loud in front of others. It can be so challenging because I need to understand, decipher and recognize the words so quickly!

The words can appear in the wrong order or all bunched together, and it can feel uncomfortable and stressful having to try to decipher the words with people listening to me.

Do you like reading out loud? Do you need time to prepare yourself or are you happy to do it at short notice? Are there books, fonts or colours you find easier to read than others?

For reading aloud, I enjoy or am good at...

When I read aloud, I really struggle to...

Reading aloud would be easier if...

What I want teachers or grown-ups to know about how reading aloud is for me

Receiving/understanding information

This is sometimes called "processing" and it is the way we receive and understand the information given to us.

I find it really difficult to process large amounts of information. I can get confused if I am not given an idea of how everything fits together. I need to know how my bit fits into all the other bits rather like a big jigsaw puzzle.

Another way of saying this is that dyslexics are often "big picture" thinkers. We need to know the gist – or overall picture – first before we can take in the detail.

What about you? Is there a particular way you like to see or hear large pieces of information or instructions? Are you good at asking for help if you need it? Do you write things down?

For processing information, I enjoy or am good at...

When I process information, I really struggle to...

Processing information would be easier if...

What I want teachers or grown-ups to know about how processing information is for me

Lots of things can help!

The good news is that there are loads of things you, and the grown-ups around you, can do to help. Perhaps you use some of these already.

Creatia's super traffic lights!

Creatia can sometimes struggle to remember all the positive things she can do. She finds it easier to think about things she finds tricky. She uses traffic lights to explain to teachers or other adults how she feels about spelling, reading, writing or listening.

Here's how she does it:

1. First draw a traffic light – a green circle, an orange circle and a red circle (don't colour them in yet – just draw the outline). We've done one for you, but it could be more fun to draw your own!

2. Next think about something you do at home or school – it could be reading, spelling, talking out loud or something else.

3. Write it down.

4. Then colour in the traffic light to show how you feel about it.

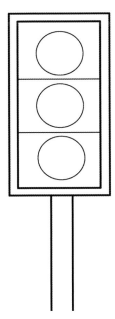

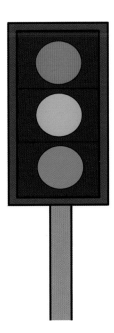

If you feel you are super-duper at spelling, for example, then colour the green traffic light. If you think you are quite good but need a bit of help, then colour the amber (orange) traffic light. If you feel as if you are really struggling, then colour the red light.

You can chat to your teacher or grown-up about what you may be finding tricky and share any ideas about what you think might help.

You can come back to these traffic lights again at a later date to see how you feel then. Have things got any easier?

Here are some tips on spelling, reading, writing or listening you can share with your grown-up to try to find a way of getting you all the way to green.

Tips on getting to green

Spelling

There are lots of different apps and games to help with reading, writing and understanding information. Many of these can be used in the classroom or to help with homework. For Creatia, b-r-e-a-k-i-n-g words or pages into manageable chunks is the key to tackling things she finds tricky. Clapping out the number of syllables or seeing smaller words within words can really help. What about hiding your words in a picture or colouring them in, or putting them on your bedroom wall so they magically drift into your brain while you are playing or sleeping?

Remember that at least one out of every ten of the world's population is dyslexic, so you are not alone. Clever, creative minds such as yours have come up with fantastic ways of teaching and helping that don't always require a pen, a piece of paper and a desk. Look online, visit the library and ask your school for ideas.

Reading

Being read to by a grown-up and reading with a classmate or friend are great ways of enjoying the story without worrying about the individual words. Audio books are a wonderful way to relax and enjoy disappearing into another world, particularly on a long car journey or before bed when you feel too tired to tackle a full page of writing in a book.

You may also benefit from coloured overlays (these are see-through coloured sheets that go over your book so you can see the letters and words more clearly).

Top tip: Read the books you enjoy. Don't worry about what anyone else is reading.

Writing

It is often the smallest things that make the biggest difference. Perhaps something as simple as a pencil grip might help. Do you ever find your hand getting tired? Bigger lines in your jotters or breaking large bits of writing down can help too. Have you tried writing with your finger in a box of sand or painting your letters? There are lots of good writing programmes and games. Maybe you do some of your writing on a computer. Or is there another way of presenting your ideas? Can you draw or talk about your ideas instead?

Listening

Grown-ups sometimes need a little reminder to break things down, and to slow down. It helps if you can understand your instructions one by one. Try your hardest to look at the person who is talking to you – this really helps.

Think about when you work best. Are you better at concentrating in the morning? If you have a piece of work to do or something to read for school, then don't try to do it when you are already tired or frustrated. Make sure you are in a good mood and are ready to give it your best.

Think about the environment – that's a big fancy word for what's around you. If it is noisy, busy or messy, it might be harder for you to focus on what you are doing. Find a space where you won't be easily distracted, or think about what you can do to help you focus. Some people prefer silence, whereas others like listening to music, for example. Some people with dyslexia use ear defenders in busy classrooms to help them to concentrate. Do you think this would work for you?

Practise

Practise. Practise. Practise. Try different ways of learning. Get up and move about. Try passing a ball to a grown-up or friend and saying a letter at a time, or using sticks or cutlery to form your letters. Hard work always pays off and will help you develop your own ways of overcoming any problems you encounter. Be creative!

Summarize what you've learned in this chapter in the box under the cartoon on the next page.

Then, as in the previous chapter, complete the superhero picture.

Finally, create your own character who shows all the amazing strategies and solutions you've come up with to tackle words!

WORDS...

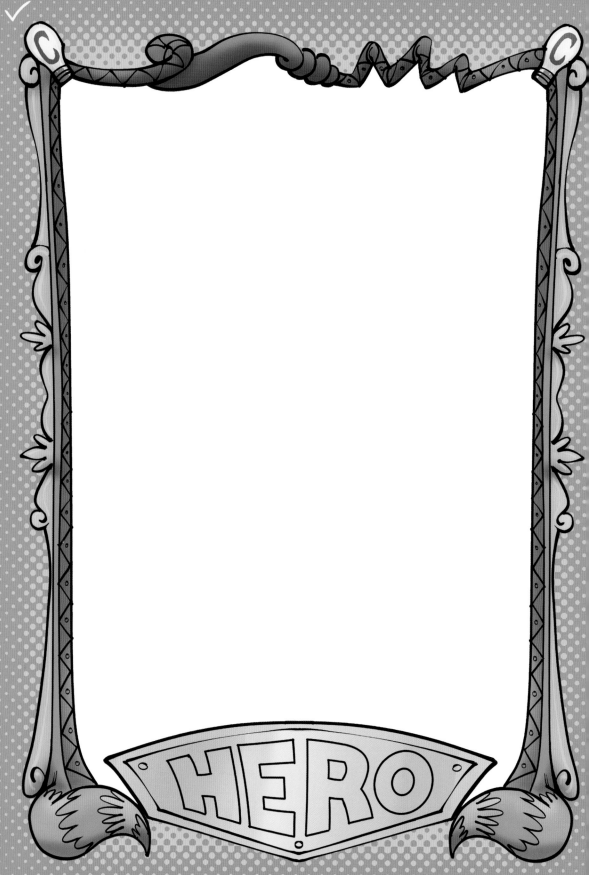

Wow! Good job in the Words chapter. See, Mr D is getting even smaller!

CHAPTER 6

Organized for Chaos

Oops! Looks as if Creatia got on the wrong bus. Perhaps she could do with a little bit of help with her organizational skills? These are the skills we develop to order and make sense of our lives so we don't have to juggle too many things all at once. They are things like remembering all the equipment we need for school (pencil case, PE kit, water bottle, lunch bag, homework) and planning out our time to make sure we are not doing everything at the last minute. It's about thinking of the equipment and strategies that will help us through the challenges of the day.

Now this one is my favourite. I particularly love it when the teacher tells you off in class for not having a pencil. Ha ha ha ha! There's nothing you can do about it!

Don't listen to him. Right, there must be something we can do. What about packing your bag the night before? Or using coloured folders to keep everything in the right place?

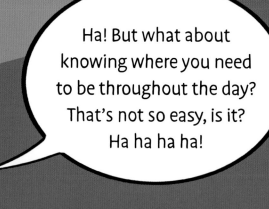

Ha! But what about knowing where you need to be throughout the day? That's not so easy, is it? Ha ha ha ha!

Well, we could use colour again. The most important thing is to never be afraid to ask for help. We don't have to figure everything out on our own. Work with other people, find something that works for you and give it your maximum effort. That's the very best anyone can expect!

There is no getting away from the fact that remembering everything you need to do and bring can feel a bit overwhelming at times but the heroes have come up with some great ideas. Maybe you have some ideas of your own already?

Have a go at designing a gadget to make sure you never forget anything – something that will keep you super organized. What skills or buttons would it have? How would it keep track of where you have to be and what you have to bring? Is it a school bag which sorts everything into the right order and knows what day you have PE? Is it a special alarm clock which tells you five minutes before you have to be anywhere? An extra arm to carry your bag? What else would be really useful for you?

On the next page create your very own super-duper "Organize me" gadget. Give it a name too.

Wow! That looks great. Well done.

Did you think about what you can do to help? What works for you? It might be packing your bag the night before, or having a calendar on the wall to remind you if you have PE or music or karate that day, or simply putting things in boxes or folders you can pick up easily.

What can others do? How can the grown-ups around you help you develop strategies to be more organized? Think about what they could do to help. Do you need a reminder to pack your bag? Or a checklist on the wall?

Being tired makes everything harder. Try your best to get a good night's sleep. Give yourself time to think. Don't try to remember everything when you are tired.

Have a go at completing the superhero in the picture on page 91.

On page 92 draw one of your own with the right gadgets to help you get super organized.

ORGANIZED CHAOS...

Look, you are working so hard being creative and persevering that
Mr D is really miserable now!

CHAPTER 7

Shake it Up!

So we've heard a lot about the things Mr D is really good at: stealing time, causing chaos, shaking words and numbers about.

What about the things YOU are good at? Could we use some of these skills to make things easier for us?

Making a comic strip or poster is a great way to complete your topic work, for example.

Ooh, I made a great poster all about ancient Egypt. It was really fun. It made it loads easier to remember as well. I like to picture things rather than learning lists of facts. It's easier for me to learn when I can make something come to life.

It's funny you should say that. My friend collects football cards, and no matter how many he has, he remembers all the players' stats and teams. He gives them all actions on an imaginary pitch and can see them in his head diving for goal or dribbling past the defenders. The numbers appear over their heads as they would in a video game. It's so cool.

That's that dyslexic super skill again, isn't it? Visual thinking. It's not just for the classroom, you know. I can't always picture something like your friend, Persisto, but I do find that if I make something fun, I am more likely to remember it. For example, I remember the points on the compass by giving each one a funny word. North, East, South, West becomes **N**aughty **E**lephants **S**quirt **W**ater. Ha ha, much more fun!

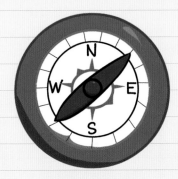

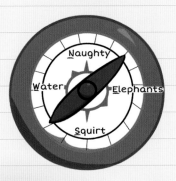

Often, making up a funny word or a song or story can help us to remember tricky facts or pieces of information. Drawing can help too. Creatia has all sorts of pictures and doodles in her jotters and notebooks or hanging on her bedroom wall. When she draws, things just make more sense.

Remember to use your dyslexic super strengths whenever you can. The more you do it, the easier things become.

Think about something you find hard to remember. It might be times tables, the 24-hour clock, your teacher's name, somebody's birthday. Try to come up with a dyslexic super-strength strategy which might help you remember it. Is it clapping it out? Making up a story or song? Drawing a picture? A funny rhyme? Passing a ball or imagining a conversation? Talk to a grown-up or family member about how you're going to do this and then try to put it into action. Did it help you?

Here are some things other children (and people who used to be children) with dyslexia have said...

Megaphone mouth

I would love an invisible megaphone to appear over my mouth when I'm reading out loud so it sounds loud and clear.

Vision goggles

I always imagine I am wearing vision goggles so I can't see the rest of the class when I am reading out loud.

Balloon popping

When I try to sound words out, I picture a clown popping balloons one by one, each one containing a bit of the word. As the balloons pop, the sounds merge together.

Glue it!

I imagine having a glue stick as an arm or leg. I can screw it off when I need to stick the words so they stay on the page.

Pause!

I would love to have ear defenders that pause and slow down the teacher's words so I can hear them again without having to ask.

Concentration hat

Imagine having a backpack that has an extendable arm, and every time I start to lose concentration it comes out and puts a hat on my head, reminding me to pay attention. That would be so cool.

Sidekick

I would love a sidekick – who floats about invisible to everyone else – and tells me I can do it when I need it.

Bye-bye negativity

Imagine having a lightsabre that cuts through any negative thoughts – that would be great!

File it away

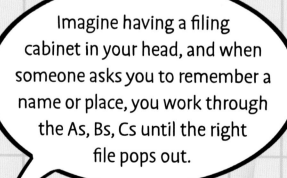

Imagine having a filing cabinet in your head, and when someone asks you to remember a name or place, you work through the As, Bs, Cs until the right file pops out.

Hang on...I'm just printing my thoughts

I always imagine having a backpack which prints out what I'm thinking so I don't need to try to get it out of my head and on to paper.

Noted

I find that when I write things down, I can't read my notes when I go back to them, so sometimes I record what's happening or take a photo of it on my phone instead.

Make it fun

I made up comics to help remember all the things I needed to learn for exams at school. I was so good at it that I do it for a job now! It made all the right things stick in place.

GLUE

Have a go at thinking of your own dyslexic strengths. What is great about you? How does your brain come up with creative solutions that other people might not have thought of?

Write your strengths under the cartoon on the next page. Then have a go at completing our superhero drawing.

And finally, if you'd like to, you can draw a superhero character with loads of dyslexic strengths!

SHAKE IT UP...

HERO

CHAPTER 8

Everything's Going to Be OK

People might tell you it is just about reading and writing, but dyslexia can affect all aspects of your life. It can affect the way you feel about yourself. This can be for a whole variety of reasons. The way a dyslexic brain processes and understands the world is different from a non-dyslexic brain. Although this can be really good sometimes, it also means that you may find yourself in situations where everybody else in your class seems to understand something more quickly than you, or instructions people give you may not make sense or can become jumbled if they are not broken down.

Have you ever been sent upstairs to get pants, socks and a T-shirt and got to your room and had no idea what you were supposed to be doing?

Or really want to know how long you've got left playing a game or doing a piece of work, but then find that if somebody says you have 20 minutes, all you do is count down the minutes without being able to do your work for fear of time running out?

If you are having difficulty understanding time, then your parent or a grown-up telling you to come home in an hour can cause more worry – meaning you can't relax and enjoy yourself. When you are waiting for your new Xbox game to load, 5 minutes can feel like an hour. Going to a party with your classmates should be fun – you should be able to do this, right? But it turns out there are too many variables and you don't understand the rules, which means you might feel worried or get into trouble.

All of this is completely normal. All our heroes have felt unsure or stressed or angry at some point in their lives too. It's important to acknowledge when things are difficult for you. As we know from reading this book, the good news is there's loads that you, and those around you, can do to help.

Time to talk

Willforce always takes time to talk. The very first thing you should do if you are worried about something is to **talk to somebody** you trust about how you are feeling. The more you, and everybody around you, understands about what is hard and easy for you, the easier it is to plan and support each other. Maybe arrange with your grown-up to give a thumbs up, middle or down about what kind of day you have had when you get in from school, or over dinner. You could also keep a notepad and pen by your bed to write or draw anything you are worried about.

Practise every day, reminding yourself of the things that went well, as well as recognizing the things that felt challenging.

You can use the space in the frame on the next page to note down the things that went well, even if these seem tiny to you.

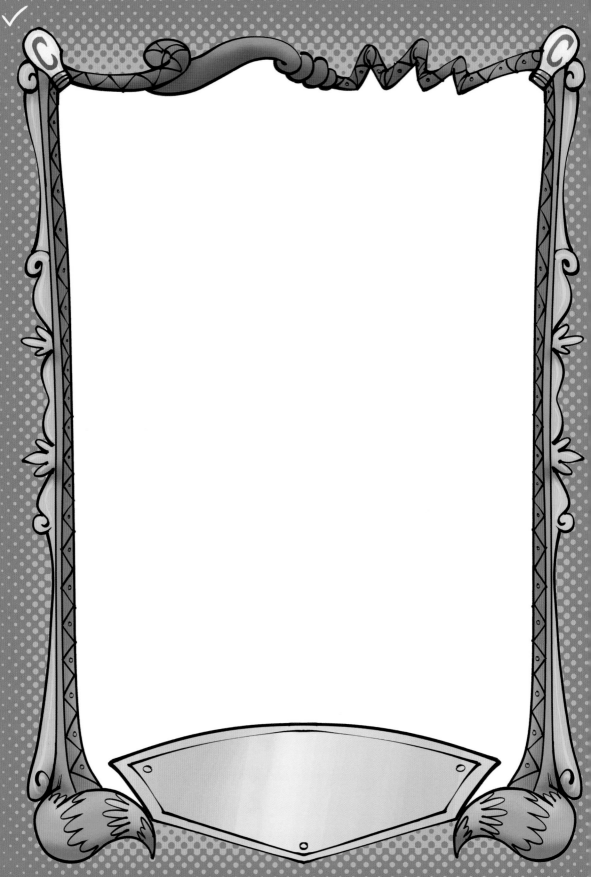

Something I did well today

You are doing so well. Chances are you are already working at least 10% harder than children in your class who are not dyslexic. The grown-ups around you know this and appreciate that it can be hard. Be good to yourself. Rest, talk, do things that you love when you come home from school. Try to get a good night's sleep, get out in the fresh air, play with your friends, eat your dinner and let go of negative experiences. Tomorrow is a brand-new day, filled with opportunities for you to shine.

It is the job of all the adults at home and school to help you find ways to cope with challenges. Often the best ideas can come from you, though. Put that wonderful dyslexic brain to work and think up clever, creative solutions to the challenges you might face.

If there were no obstacles or barriers in your way, what would you like to do in ten years' time? Talk to a grown-up or family member about it.

- Where would you live?

- Would it be hot and sunny or cold and snowy?

- Who would be there?

- What would you be doing every day?

- What would you eat for breakfast?

Here's your chance to bring together all the brilliant skills and knowledge you have gained by reading this book.

It's your chance to design your very own superhero like Creatia, Persisto and Willforce.

How will your hero help you with any challenges you face because of your dyslexia?

How big is your superhero? What's their favourite colour?

Do they have a name?

What special gadget can you invent for them to help you with stuff you maybe find tricky – such as words, time, organization or believing in yourself? (If you need to, you can have a look back at the end of Chapter 7 for some ideas from other dyslexic children – and adults! – about gadgets your unique superhero could have.)

Do they have some of your dyslexic superpowers?

Are they creative or sporty or a great friend?

Draw your hero, with their superpowers and their helpful gadget in the frame on the next page. Then ask a grown-up to take a picture of them and tweet it to @JKPBooks and @DyslexiaMission so we can see your fantastic superheroes in action.

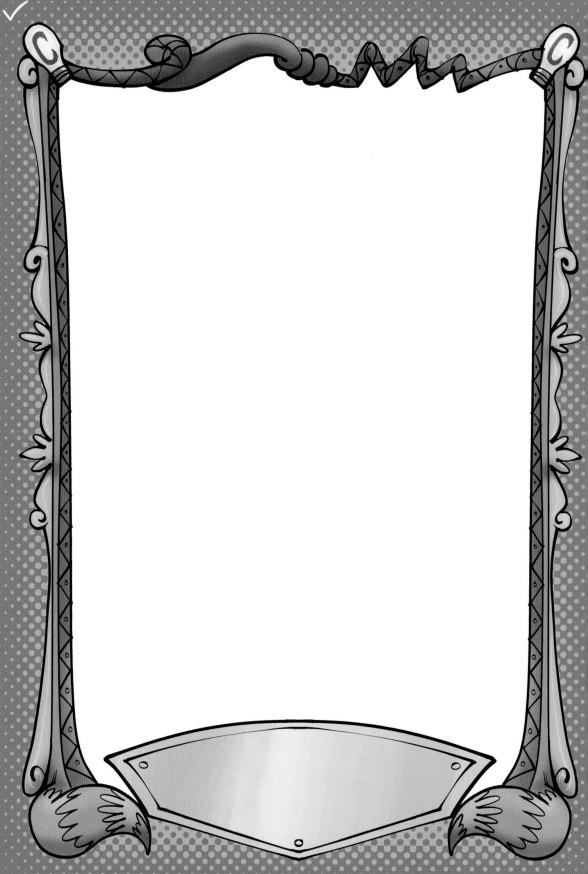

You've got this!

Never forget the super skills you have.

Always ask for help.

Know that, when things get tough,
the heroes are all around you.

Go forward and shine like the bright star you are.

CHAPTER 9

The Stuff Grown-Ups Should Know

Warning! Kids may find this chapter a bit dull and boring – you can skip it if you like. This bit has homework for grown-ups in it!

We would encourage parents and teachers and support staff to really talk together, and with dyslexic children themselves, to find out what might work best for the child – and use this book as a prompt for discussion.

On the next few pages, you will find some specific tips and words of encouragement addressed to teachers and parents.

Please do read both sections, as we can all learn from adopting one another's point of view sometimes.

For the superhero teachers, support staff and leaders: You've got this!

- Thank you for reading this book.

- Thank you for working hard every day for children who live with learning differences. You are changing lives, I promise you.

- Please remember that children with dyslexia are often working much harder than other children in your class, even if it doesn't always seem that way, and they are often exhausted because of this.

- You already know you need to differentiate work and adapt the way you deliver instructions to dyslexic children in your classroom, even those who look as if they are coping.

- Praise, praise, praise. Praise effort, praise difference and praise bravery. Children with dyslexia are much more likely to suffer from low self-esteem. They may need your praise more than most.

- Is there anything you can do to improve the classroom environment? Can everyone see you/the board? Are there quiet spaces or visual aids? Are there resources that would enhance everyone's learning experience?

- Learning aids: Children say they like it if ear defenders, pencil grips, coloured overlays are made available for ALL children in the classroom. This normalizes difference and makes it easier for everyone to get the support or help they need.

- Teamwork: Often everyone has a piece of the jigsaw. Learning plans should be developed alongside all teachers, support staff and specialists working with the child, parents and, most importantly, the child themselves. Keep checking in because things change quickly at home and at school. Include classroom assistants and learning support workers – they hold vital insight into what works and what doesn't.

- Find a way of planning with a child that minimizes the time they have to be called out of class. Often they never really catch up on what was lost in that time and most don't like attending countless meetings with grown-ups and teachers. Is there another way of capturing their views?

- Dyslexia is a complex shape-shifter and often comes hand in hand with other learning differences or conditions. Something that worked for one child last year might not work again.

- Think carefully before asking a dyslexic child to stay in at break or lunch because they haven't completed a piece of work. Balance the need to support the child to focus on the task in hand with their very real need for time to relax, regroup and process everything that happened that morning.

- Make it normal. Not just dyslexia – make "difference" normal. And not just "normal" – make it something to be celebrated. Remind your class and your school that they are all stronger because of this difference, that the world would be boring if we were all the same and that everybody has their own strengths.

- Be a champion. Attend the training, organize the parent groups, facilitate the assemblies, wear the blue ribbon. Be the person who makes children proud to be dyslexic – this confidence might just be the thing they carry with them throughout the challenges ahead.

- Use technology in the classroom and beyond. Help your dyslexic children to find ways of unlocking their wonderful, creative minds beyond the blank page.

- Celebrate achievements beyond the school gates.

- Set realistic goals and talk about role models who have dyslexia.

- Talk to parents. Parents worry about their dyslexic children. Let them know what they can do to support their children's learning at home.

For the superhero parents and carers: You've got this!

- It's tough. We know it, you know it. Dyslexia can be like an additional member of your family, bringing with it all the joy, attention, demands and rewards any other new addition brings.

- It takes time to get used to. It demands trial and error, and there will be challenges and rewards for each and every family member when dyslexia is present in your lives.

- It is important to take time to talk about the challenges dyslexia presents within your household.

- Think about how you can alter or adapt your environment to make things easier for all. At home, where does your child do homework? Make sure that wherever they are studying, they can access the materials they need easily. Is it noisy or busy? Is there an adult available to ask for help?

- Make sure each person in the household has the opportunity to thrive, even if this means providing opportunities outside the classroom. Make sure you celebrate the successes and display your child's work and commend their achievements.

- Keep going. Keep learning about your child, about dyslexia, about things you can do to support their self-esteem and development. Try new things and acknowledge when you get it wrong. There is no "one size fits all".

- Don't worry about being "that parent" at your child's school. Sometimes you need to fight and sometimes you need to reach across the divide and bring people with you. You are the parent who is making a difference and nothing is more important than that. Listen to the teachers and remember they are doing their best. Work together to find solutions wherever possible.

- Trust your instincts. You will come up with your own ways of working that suit your family and the dyslexic child.

- Write things down – things that worked, things you raised with your child's school/educational psychologist/education authority, dates of meetings and actions agreed, websites and resources and where to find them. Share this information with your child's school.

- Whatever strategies you develop, a degree of separation between home and school is often very important. Home can be that safe space where your child can let go of all the things that have been challenging during the day. Learning in a classroom can be really challenging for your dyslexic child because of the way their brain processes and understands information, and this may show in their behaviour or in how they feel about themselves.

- You will need a truckload of patience (but you know that already) –

patience dispelling the myths to others, patience explaining your child's dyslexia (again) to people working with them, patience with your child when all your strategies work one day and none the next, and, lastly, patience with yourself. You've got this – you are doing great!

- Remember always, always, that you are not alone. Ask for help!

- One in ten (at least) of the population is dyslexic. Seek out support and be that hand of friendship to others. The school years can be tough, but a child's dyslexia will offer them many opportunities and may just be the thing that helps them shine.

When we work together

It's important for us all to think about the challenges too. Spend some time writing them down or talking with the child and/or another teacher, or your partner or friend about the things that are tough and what you could put in place to make things easier.

The important thing to remember is that your coping strategies are yours: they will be hard-won and specific to you and your family or a child's class.

Have a go at thinking about some rules/mantras you can put in place in your household and/or at school to help deal with any challenges that may come your way. At home, these should apply to the whole family, and, in the classroom or group, to all the children.

You thought you were getting out of the exercises, didn't you?

Put each strategy/tip on Willforce's shield in the illustration on page 123.

At home, these could be things like "Have dinner together" or "Homework-free night on Wednesday". At school or home they could be "Tell each other three things about our day", "Describe someone who helped us today" or "Talk about someone we helped out with something today".

Find out what works for you.

It's important to remember that all children need opportunities to succeed. No matter how far we think we have come, often these opportunities come outside of the classroom, or outside the realm of academic learning, for many children with dyslexia.

Keep the child at the centre – ask them what excites them.

Research extracurricular or lunchtime clubs and activities and see what's going on. Are there any good art classes/computer clubs/netball teams? It doesn't matter so much what the activity is, but it matters how it makes them feel. The structure and routine will be worth 1000 internet searches into handwriting skills. Don't worry if your child appears to be wary of new activities or is lacking in confidence.

Parents or support staff: It's OK if they need you more than their friends seem to need their parents or grown-ups. They will get there; it might just take a little longer for them to process all the variables in a new situation. You are not "babying" them if you are the only parent at the side of the football pitch or gymnastics practice. Take your lead from your child; they will let you know when they are ready to fly.

Separation between home and school is very important, and this is something that teachers can be aware of too.

Sometimes school can be really tough and stressful for a dyslexic child. They may be working much, much harder than their peers and still not achieving what they would like to achieve.

They may become frustrated or withdrawn, and chances are that parents will get the brunt of that as parents are the child's "safe place" – a place for them to be themselves at the end of a challenging day.

If they do have a hard time at school or make a mistake, try to leave that mistake at school or in the classroom.

Try not to punish a child by keeping them off art class or computer club. Those extracurricular activities might be the only thing making a dyslexic child feel good about themselves that week.

Self-esteem is fragile and is the key to building resilience and success.

Keep talking.

It sounds obvious but dyslexia is a shape-shifter. You need to be on your toes, equipped with new strategies for each new situation. Your child is the expert on their dyslexia. Listen to them.

Parents and teachers: Find a tribe. Attend the masterclasses, start a support group in your school, call the helplines, research, find all the resources, become a champion for dyslexia. It really will help. Never forget how valuable you are. Your experience is vital for others. You are the most important advocates for a dyslexic child. Keep fighting the fight or providing the shoulder to cry on. You are the real superheroes in a child's life. Mr D is no match for you! Good luck with your journey. We are all behind you.

Other JKP children's books about dyslexia

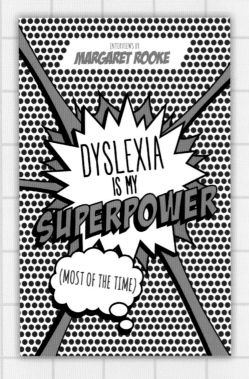

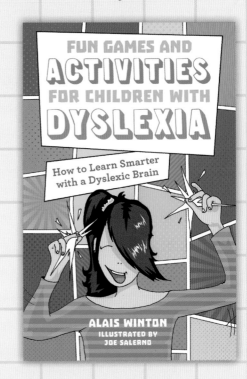

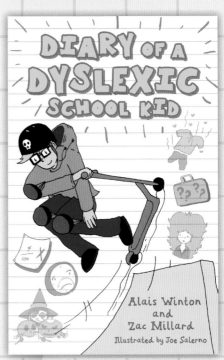

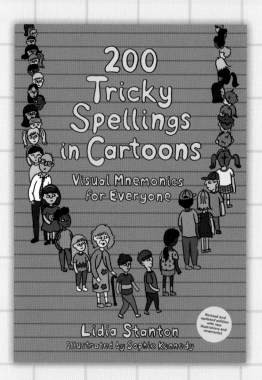

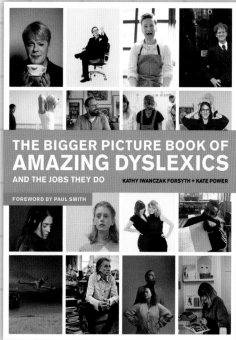